SKILLS TO SELF DEVELOPMENT

A GUILD TO PERSONAL GROWTH AND DEVELOPMENT

EMMA PENTOOL

ISBN: 9798843838317

DEDICATION

This book is dedicated to all young teens and adults, who are seeking for ways to improve on their personal growth and development in other to be of positive value to the society

CONTENTS

RELATIONSHIP SKILLS

First let us consider relationship. As we grow older daily, we come across different kinds of people in the environment or society in which we inhabit, who we interact, transact business and associate with. We relate with them irrespective of the educational, religious, social, political and cultural backgrounds. This makes relationship broader, as we not only know and meet our family members, we meet, relate and transact with the wider society.

By definition, relationship is a social bond or attachment between two or more persons. It is the basis of human interaction, the expression of love and intimacy without exploitation or manipulation. It is the way or manner people feel and behave towards each or one another. It is also a close friendship between two or more people. It is a way in which they are connected.

One would wonder how the nature of these relationships are, they are basically in two forms, that is, relationship with the family and relation with the larger society

* **Relationship with the family:** This comprises of the father, mother and the children. This is known as nuclear family. Again, we also have extended family which comprises of our uncles, aunties, cousins, nephews, nieces, grandparents etc.

* **Relationship with the larger society:** This comprises of individual persons like our teachers, fellow students, doctors, nurses, drivers, pilots, pastors, engineers, politicians, security officials etc. and with members of groups or associations, age grades, school authority, clubs and societies, etc. Importantly, life style of youths in today's trend is that they negotiate and enter into different types of relationships. Although, this is normal, youths and teens must be careful and guided to set limits in any type of relationship they may enter or form with one another

The Family

Now, the family comprised of people related by blood, marriage or law. It is the basic unit of the society that bears the responsibilities of supporting, caring and preparing the children for adulthood. As noted earlier this family could be extended or nuclear. The extended family is the commonest family type in Nigeria comprising in most cases of the father/husband, mother/wife, children, grandparents, uncles, aunties and cousins etc. The nuclear family on the other hand, includes the father/husband, mother or mothers/ wife or wives, step mother, step father, step daughters, and step sons (the children). Where polygamy exists, we have co-wives, step mother(s), step father(s), step children etc. as part of this structure. Another interesting type of family becoming common in these changing world or times is the 'foster family' as a result of many children becoming orphans early in life and such have to be catered for. Another reason for this is economic hardship. The difference between fostering and adoption is that, adoption is usually by legal action in which case adopted children are given the rights of children born into that family. Whereas, fostering is the giving of alms or succor to the abandoned, orphan, less privilege or needy.

However, every family has its uniqueness and differences. These are seen in their viz:

- Personalities.
- Physical attributes.
- Talents.
- Riches and affluence.
- Interests and values.
- Strengths and weaknesses.

Again, every member of the family has a role and responsibility. For instance, our parents have the responsibilities to provide love, food, clothes, shelter, pay our fees and bills and most importantly be our guardians. On the -other hand, children on their own part are to be obedient, respectful, assist in house-hold chores and other domestic activities (very important), as well as do well in school as they prepare their lives into a meaningful adulthood. As children 8advance to adolescent, (teen) and youthful age, changes occur in their families. Some of these changes include:

• Increase sense of responsibilities.

• Heightened sense of independence.

• Tendency to spend more time with non-family members or law. It is

• Tendency to be secretive or confidential.

Nevertheless, these actions have implications some of which include:

a. **Conflict:** This result when one party or person perceives that his/her interest is threatened or in contradiction with the goals or values of another person. It is a state of disagreement or hostility where one out of the two or more parties strives to gain advantage or have his/her way or say id mother in a matter of interest. Conflict according to Aristotle is inevitable in and step human relationships or interactions. Like a universal saying "you disagree 8to agree." Conflict resolutions strategies are therefore very important in this factor to maintain and/or retain relationships and also ensure that relationships are cordial and harmonious. Because the way or manner conflicts are handled could make or mar relationships, it could either be changing constructive or destructive.

b. **Anger:** This is a strong feeling of displeasure, rage, or fury. It is a natural for this is instinct inherent in the lives of human beings. It is a biological process that cannot be avoided. However, its exhibition or exercise is paramount in a relationship. At a particular stage of our lives, there are vital and urgent needs for us to examine, understand and know our temperaments to enable us have firm control of our lives and situations around us. Every human being is naturally endowed to exercise his/her anger but the way or manner it is exhibited matters tremendously in a relationship. As learned persons, we ought to/should have firm control of anger so that we don't cause grievous harm to ourselves, loved ones and people around us. Even Solomon; the wises man that ever lived warned through divine inspiration that "You should not be hot-tempered or make friends with a hot-tempered persons, or associate with someone who is easily angered, so that you don't learn their ways and get yourself ruined." Anger destroys relationships, so you should be cautious to exercise or exhibit it. Retain or maintain good and harmonious relationships.

c. **Callousness:** This is very destructive in relationships. It is lack of feelings, empathy and insensitivity to others. It is expression of lack of love and care to the needs of others. Love is a strong feeling of caring for one another. Children of God will love one another. It is a gift to those who are willing to receive and give it. It is selfless and enables us to care for ourselves and neighbors. In expressing or showing love to one another, sincerity, fairness and honesty are the principal principles. This love is agape, divine and unconditional. It is not canal (sexual immorality) or selfish. It is the love that made God gave us His only begotten Son to redeem us from eternal destruction. You must love one another; for this is the greatest command. Shone callousness for it destroys.

d. **Jealousy:** This does not build relationships nor encourage harmonious relationships. It is anger, dissatisfaction or displeasure expressed because of what your friend, brother, sister or neighbor has, bought, given or achieved. It is envy and inability to appreciate others for what they have or have attained. It is important to note that what you don't appreciate you cannot have. When you appreciate and congratulate people for the success or favor they have, you are subconsciously or indirectly paving way for your own turn. What you celebrate, you attract. Remember, 'one good turn deserves another.' If your own has not happened, relax do not be dismayed, it will surely come. Weeping may endure for a night but joy will surely come in the morning. So rejoice and celebrate with others when good or great things happen to them.

e. **Misunderstanding:** This severely causes conflicts in relationships. It is caused as a result of impaired communication consequent upon lack of focus or listening or misinterpretation of communication either verbally or non-verbally. Effective and efficacious communication is vital to building strong relationships. There is need for communication, understanding and feedback for relations to thrive. People perish for lack of knowledge and understanding. Get wisdom; get understanding for they are principal to the issues of life.

f. Fear: 'False Evidence Appearing Real'. This happens as a result of distrust. When family members lose trust in themselves, fear intrudes. Ordinarily, it ought not to be so. This fear can sometimes manifest in form of financial insecurity, life insecurity, property insecurity, etc. Fear is eschewed when there are love, sincerity, honesty, care and effective communication.

g. **Exploitation:** This is concerned with using a person unfairly for personal benefit. It is a danger signal in a relationship. On certain occasions everyone uses other people, however, continually doing so unduly, poisons a relationship. Exploiters tend to be selfish, with little trust in others. They often have little feeling for fairness and feel no guilt when they don't fill commitments. Exploiters believe that everyone is out to get the maximum, so they use others before others use them.

Interestingly, there are therapeutic factors that enhance good family relationships, they include:

- Taking responsibility for one's action and caring for one another.
- Effective communication.
- Involvement of everyone (family members) especially the discerning minds in decision making.
- Loving and expressing compassion to one another.
- Recognizing and respecting family values.
- Being honest, faithful and sincere.
- Respecting individual rights including the rights of children.
- Encouraging and exhibiting positive values.
- Being nice and exhibiting right or good attitude.
- Good conflict resolution strategy; embracing and encouraging dialogue, peace and tolerance.

The Larger Society

Every time you make a connection with another person, a relationship forms or establishes. Some relationships are voluntary, that is, you choose them. Others, such as those with most family members and people in the school, are involuntary. They are not chosen. Family relationships as discussed earlier will like to be among the most important ones you ever have. Few bonds are stronger than those between family members. Most people have relationships that extend beyond the family. They need friends too. Friendships include people of all ages and backgrounds. Some are much closer than other. Beyond family and friends, people have many casual relationships. A need for others, some people need more relationships in life than others do. A person who is very social may want a wide circle of friends. Another person may need fewer relationships to be happy. More important than quantity is quality. Relationships should be satisfying. When relationships are positive, they serve some important purposes or functions in your life. First, your emotional needs are met. Through family and friends, you feel loved and accepted. Relationships also enrich lives as people share experiences, feelings, ideas, and ideals. Not only do others contribute to your life, bus contribute to others as well. Finally, relationships help you get things done. What you accomplish is often related to the help and support you get/have from others.

"We must learn to live together as brothers/sisters or perish together as fools." - Martin Luther King, Jnr

Factors That Make Relationships Work

You need to know the behavior and traits of people in other to relate to them appropriately. Let us examine some of the 'A' factors that enhance relationships:

• Association

• Assessment

• Appreciation

• Advancement

• Assistance

• Acceptance

• Agreement

Association

As the saying goes "A tree does not make a forest." The word 'associate' implies that you have a desire to work and relate with other people. You may not often have the privilege of associating with people of 'like minds', but the important thing is to look for people who have 'minds that you like'. Such people may disagree with you, but they are positive and open minded. According to Seyi Wright (2007), four important principles will serve as a guide when 'associating' or relating with people Wisdom, Persistence, Tact and Innocence.

It is good to be wise and sharp or 'smart' in a positive sense in dealing with people, but you should be innocent in your intentions. Since most people have their own personal agenda, you need to be tactful and persistent when relating to them; always striving to maintain your focus on genuinely making a difference in their lives.

Assessment

We should all know that we do not 'Judge a book by the cover', yet we easily jump to conclusions about others. To assess someone is to carefully study or examine that person until you have got a good understanding of him/her. This is achieved through a desire to understand, observe, dialogue, and feedback. Your effectiveness in assessing others is also based on good understanding of yourself. Your opinion of certain people may change completely when you get to know them better, discovering that they have had some tough times or experiences which have occasioned or shaped their attitudes and actions.

Appreciation

Someone once said, "The deepest principle in human nature is the craving to be appreciated." If you are able to genuinely satisfy this craving in others, then you would have succeeded in creating a platform for better relationships. To appreciate someone is to increase the 'value' of the person, both from the person's perspective and your point of view. The point becomes clearer if you think about the fact that appreciation is the opposite of depreciation. Appreciation involves giving appropriate recognition, reward and showing fairness and justice to others. Saying thank you to what is done for you means that you acknowledge what is done for you. Most of us desire to be appreciated, but are not ready or willing to first extend to others what we desire. We therefore, make ourselves very unhappy expecting, unrealistically that the world would do our bidding. It is an unrealistic thought because other people are also looking for someone that will appreciate them. Remember, when you appreciate someone who did good/well to you, you encourage him/her to do better next time. It is interesting to note that the greatest beneficiary of appreciation is the giver.

Advancement

"My best friend is the one who brings out the best in me."

One of the greatest gifts you can give to someone else is to uplift the person's thinking ability. You 'advance' people by developing their strengths and encourage them to overcome their weaknesses. I have heard people say that they could only relate and associate with people who contribute positively to their lives and shone those who contribute nothing or rather influence them negatively. Therefore, it is expedient and encouraging to create positive impressions and influences on people.

Acceptance

Your ability to accept people for who they are makes it easier to grow sound relationships. This means that you are willing to understand certain people's idiosyncrasies, live with them and help them, with minimal stress and disagreement. When you accept and understand people, it enhances cordial and harmonious relationships.

Agreement

"We should not seek to forget our differences; rather we should strive to understand them." - Sir Ahmadu Bello

To agree is to gain an understanding and appreciation of the position of others, which requires conscious effort. There is a need to understand the personalities and behavior of others. It is hard work, yes! But the task is inevitable. We may feel too busy, too stressed, too broke or too frustrated by the situations or circumstances around us to empathize with others. Thereby denying ourselves of opportunities to relate better and strengthen our relationship in many situations. However, sincerity should underlie our motives in relating to others.

Relationship Qualities

What makes a relationship a good one? Several qualities can be singled out or examined as keys to good relationships, especially those of family and friends.

1. **Mutuality:** A good relationship is mutual. It means both or among people contributes to the feelings and actions that support the relationship. They know and understand what they want from each other or one another. The closer a relationship, the more willing people are to give without expecting something in return.

2. **Trust:** The belief that others will not reject, betray or hurt you is called trust. Acceptance and support are part of trusting. Trust is needed in all relationships, regardless of how close they are. Friends and family members trust one another not to reveal confidential information.

3. **Self-Disclosure:** To build close relationships, people have learnt to share themselves with others. Self-disclosure means telling others about you. The ability to disclose information about you at least to one person (your mummy, daddy, pastor, role model, or trusted relative or friend) is very important for good mental

health. However, how much information a person discloses is significant. In the strongest, closest relationships, people feel free to talk about their fears, anger, hope, ideals, beliefs, joy and grieve.

4. **Rapport**: In good relationships, people have rapport with one another. It is a feeling of ease and harmony with another person.

5. **Empathy:** When you have the ability to put yourself in another person's situation or position you have empathy for that person(s). You try to set aside your own ideas and understand others point of views.

6. **Shared Interest**: Relationships survive better or thrive when at least some interests are shared. You probably know the feeling with someone who has no interests like yours, you have little to talk about or do together. Someone who shares your interests and values will respect you and respect them and would not attempt to force or propel you to do or act contrary to your values. When you meet someone who has or shares a special interest with you, however, the bond is there. You have a strong base for building a relationship.

7. **Respect:** To respect means to honor, to hold in high regard or esteem; to treat others as worthwhile even when the person is different from you, to obey and reverence, parents, elderly persons, constituted authorities, rules and regulations.

8. **Being Responsible**: To be responsible means that others can depend on you, that is, you are reliable, that you can fulfill your obligations and will be able to distinguish right from wrong.

9. **Understanding:** To understand means to be knowledgeable about another person, his/her temperament. What he/she wants and needs. Understanding a person could also mean to understand his/her feelings. It also means being able to put yourself in someone else's position and imagine what life looks from another person's perspective.

10. **Labor:** This means to work hard or put extra effort to make relationships work to the mutual benefits of the parties. There is an adage in my place that says "The workable relationship of two persons is made possible by one of them." Another one says "The amiable and harmonious relationship of two persons is achieved as a result of tolerance and disregard or overlook of errors and imperfection." Apparently, for relationships to work is the responsibility of someone and that person is you!

11. **Nice Attitude:** To be nice means to have a winning attitude. Any nicety that does not have winning attitude is a waste of attitude. Nice attitude makes you a winner, a champion and a success. Attitude is very essential to the success of a person. Your success in life is determined by or is a product of your attitude. It is also the right attitude that makes you stay on top. Your attitude is your true self; it is your inner self. It is what people see, it speaks more of you than what you say about yourself", it speaks more than your voice. Like a universal saying "Your attitude determines your altitude." How far you will go in life is a function of your attitude. It could either be an asset or a liability for you. Your attitude determines your relationship with others.

However, it may interest you to know that while good attitude advances and takes you to the top, bad attitude might do the contrary. Some bad attitudes include: inability to say I am sorry to a wrong done to someone; inability to forgive others that wronged or trespassed against you; critical spirit or mind (like to criticize, always looking for fault(s) in others and looking down on people); desire to take all the glory (it is only me); shifting blame (inability or unwilling to take responsibility); easily suspicious; abusive; pride; inability to keep secret etc. Your attitude is your choice.

Very importantly, to avoid conflict in relationships, youths and teens must observe some limits or boundaries. In other words, boundaries should be established in any or every relationship unless otherwise. Some rules that help set limits include:

• Agree on how the relationship will be maintained either in words or in body language. And possibly state what you expect from each other.

• Respect one another's beliefs, principles and values.

• Having right thinking; positive thinking, look at the bright side of life.

• Establish mutual trust and honesty; don't tell lies, be reliable, and trusted.

• Humble yourself and listen, to others.

• Agree ahead of time, the level of physical contact. This is important because there are some undesirable or unscrupulous behavior that may negatively affect relationships among youths and teens. Such behavior include:

a. Forceful hugging.

b. Pinching someone's buttocks or breast.

c. Forcing the opposite sex to sit on your lap (s) .

d. Hanging out with opposite sex in solitary and/or dark places at deserted or lonely places. e. Forcing or inducing a friend or person to use or abuse drugs. f. Influencing or propelling a person or friend to indulge in alcohol, or worse still drugging a person to his/her unconsciousness or oblivion.

Walking Away

Not every relationship is meant to be kept. Many can help you, but others are just the opposite. Some people just let relationships 'happen.' They forget that voluntary relationships are chosen ones. You don't need people in your life who use you, intimidate you, cause problems, or hurt you in some 8way. Your duty is to decide when it is in your best interest to walk away from a relationship.

Summarily, relationship is a human activity that is inevitable in every human endeavor. No man is an Island: Two cannot work together except they are in agreement. Relationship is a social bond or attachment between two or more people. It is the basis of human interaction, the expression of love, friendship and intimacy without exploitation or manipulation. Relationship is an important aspect of growing up and youths need to understand the criteria (conditions) for establishing relationships as well as the boundaries that need to be set during relationships in order to maintain healthier life and living positive.

(Blessed is the man that works not in the counsel or group of the ungodly, or stand in the way of sinners or sit in the seat of the scornful). - Psalm1:1

DECISION MAKING SKILLS: QUALITY CHOICES

"I will get ready and then perhaps my chance will Come!" - Abraham Lincoln

Decision making is the process of choosing one alternative from among a set of natural alternatives. This in essence, means tha8t, for decision making to exist, there must be two or more alternatives. It is the act of making up one's mind on an issue or a thing. Decision making is a frequent activity and examples include deciding on a career, deciding on activities and programs order to realize your career objectives or goals, deciding on the type or caliber of friends to keep, deciding on a particular lifestyle to live etc.

Daily living requires making hundreds of decisions. The small ones are most common. Many are so simple that they are made routinely, with little or no effort by the decider. Your family must decide at a certain stage what you eat, where you go, what you watch, the friends you make/keep etc. These and many other decisions like them are so minor that it doesn't really matter how they are made.

Despite their simplicity, small decisions can cause problems. Have you ever heard anyone say, "Don't make a mountain out of a mole hill. The message is, "Don't make more of something, than what is really is." When people spend too much time worrying about small decisions, they may overlook the bigger decisions that need to be made or taken. How do you know whether or not a decision is an important one? The answer is important. Some decisions have a greater impact, or effect, on your life than others do. Because some decisions have a great deal, not every decision can be handled with the same level of care. The greater the impact, the more there is need to spend time, thought and energy in making the decision.

As you sharpen your decision-making skills, learn to recognize what is important and what is not. How would you rank the decisions in the following list: Little or no impact, moderate impact, or high impact?

- Choosing a career
- Choosing a friend
- Deciding what courses to take in high school
- Choosing a book to read
- Deciding how much time to spend with family and friends
- Deciding whether or not to use drugs and alcohol.

Youths in today's world are exposed and influenced by a lot of factors like dirty home movies, uncensored music that plays negative roles in the lives of youths, pornographic media (electronic and print), peer pressure, corrupt values, get-rich-quick syndrome, Internet scam, wild behavior of our models and so many other (negative) vices in our society that could affect our decision making. And the choices we make have serious attendant consequences in our entire lives, such decision could make or mar us. It is therefore, imperative that we think carefully of a decision, before we make or take them. The reasons for decisions may include the following:

- To help one to accomplish one's goals.
- To determine one's position on an issue.
- To guide the action one takes so as to reduce the possibilities of regret.

Moral Decisions

Some decisions have a special dimension. They deal with matters of right and wrong, called moral decisions, these can have a strong impact in your life. Having strong principled values would help you face moral decisions.

Steps in Decision Making

There are several separate steps in decision making, they include:

1. Recognizing and defining the situation when a decision has to be taken. An effective and serious student should be able to anticipate major decision situation so as not to be caught unaware.

2. Developing alternative courses of action to deal with the situation. It is generally useful to design the process in such a way that obvious, standard, creative, innovative solutions are created as alternatives.

3. Evaluation of alternatives:- Each alternative is evaluated or assessed to determine its feasibility and consequences.

4. Selecting the best alternative: It is likely that two or more alternatives will remain, even though many alternatives will not 'sail through' the triple test of feasibility, satisfaction and affordability. Choosing the best of these alternatives is the real crux of the decision making process. It is therefore, pertinent to choose the alternative with the highest level of feasibility, satisfaction and affordability.

5. Implementing the chosen alternative: A student who has effectively and timely planned his/her career should be able to know how to effectively and efficiently apply the decision taken without deviation or undue influence from anybody irrespective of status or position. He/she should be firm and ready to achieve set goals.

6. Follow up and evaluation: A student should be sure to evaluate the effectiveness and workability of his/her decision. That is, he/she should be sure that the alternative chosen in '4' above and implemented in '5' accomplished desired result. This is more realistic in short term goal. A student can be able to evaluate himself/herself in tests, projects and examinations.

Quality Choices

"The test of our progress is not whether we add more to the abundance of those who have much; is it whether we provide enough for those who have little." - Franklin Delano Roosevelt

1. **Choice I:** I choose to understand who I am and consistently improve. You are honest with yourself about your current state (i.e. who you are, your personality and character) and consistently strive to improve, to become who you desire or aspire to be.

2. **Choice II:** I choose to elevate my maximum attainable level. You diligently strive to achieve your desired goals to ensure that you move to elevate your maximum attainable level.

3. **Choice III:** I choose to be principled. You develop a set of guiding principles which enable you to make a difference. Principles that will make you unique, that when you act or talk you are respected by both your peers and your seniors.

4. **Choice IV:** Choose to take charge of your emotions by "leading them" rather than allowing them to lead you, especially; our female folk should try as much as they can to take firm control of their emotions. As studies have it that women are emotionally weaker than their male counter-part, I have seen women of substance and class who overcame these so called "weak emotion" and achieved their nurtured dream and aspiration. Lead your emotions and your vision will be accomplished.

'The world is moving so fast these days that the man who says it can't be done is generally interrupted by someone doing it" - Harry Emerson

5. **Choicc V:** I choose to be an excellent steward. You develop the conviction to

be responsible and disciplined, accountable for the resources that have been made available to you. This will improve your personality and make you a better person.

6. **Choice VI:** I choose to think about what I think about. You develop "right thinking" continuously striving to improve the way you think to become more objective in making good decisions. And this is achievable when you engage quality study, reading widely, making consultations and researches to gain knowledge, because it is the principal thing. According to Henry Ford, ***"Thinking is the hardest work there is which probably is the reason so few engage in it".***

7. **Choice VII:** I choose to regard people as more important than my task. Your priority should be on building better relationships with people even as you effectively perform your task (Study). In other words, your domestic works, studies and religious activities should not deprive you from respecting, caring and maintaining your harmonious and cordial relationship with your parents, friends and peers. This really defines who you are.

8. **Choice VIII:** I choose to behave assertively to make a difference. You are assertive in the way you behave, which enables you to achieve better results in relating to people and positively impacting their lives. As noted earlier in the course of this study, your assertiveness would guarantee your satisfaction and simultaneously, satisfy the needs of others. You are not seen or perceived as selfish. Your assertiveness uniquely distinguishes you from your peers.

9. **Choice Ix:** I choose to communicate to make a difference. You concentrate on expressing empathy through the different ways you communicate, thus achieving great results with and through other people. Your utterances should be guided by your principles and remember that you are defined by what you say. It is not what enters into a man that defiles him; rather it is what comes out of his month.

10. **Choice X:** I choose to develop my spiritual intelligence. You are in touch with the controller of the "Control tower". Spiritual matters and growth is cross-cultural, and does not have age limit. It is boundless and profits more when we realize our spiritual commitment and works towards growth and perfection.

These ten QUALITY CHOICES are interdependent, so an enhancement of any one aspect automatically has a positive impact on the others. The first six are specifically related to your personal growth since it is crucial that you grow before you can help others to grow. The next three affirmations are directly linked to your relationship with others, while the last one relates to your spiritual intelligence.

Making Good Decisions

a) It is important for one to clarify his/her values i.e. understand and be sure of personal and family values as a basis for good decision making. This is more realistic if a student or teenager is able to observe and find out from his/her parents what the family values are, in addition to personal values, one can make good and workable decision.

b) Prior to making an important decision, it is important to have enough facts or information about all aspects of the issue in order to weigh the options and make an informed decision. This is because a decision made on incomplete or shallow information can be regrettable and dangerous to an innocent student. Therefore, decision on who become your friends, the places you go, who you spent your time with, who advises you, activities and program you indulge in, how you take your studies etc. should be thoughtfully and tactfully made.

c) It is also very necessary to think critically and determine how to make the most effective use of one's opinions and values so as to bring about a good result.

Factors That Affect Decision Making

So many things affect decisions that you are often unaware of what affect your decisions, knowing them could help you recognize those factors that sway your thinking. You can be better prepared to control them instead of letting them control you. Here are some influences on decisions. Can you think of any others?

- Religion

- Society
- Government Policy (ies)
- Family values
- Environment
- Personal preferences
- Friends
- Available information
- Feeling about Yourself
- Resources
- Pressure
- Needs and Wants
- Values

a. **Religion**: This has a way of influencing people's decision making because we are guided by the commandments and instructions from the bible or Koran. Religious doctrines also impacts human lives, as we make decisions that do not contradict our beliefs and doctrines taught to us by our pastors, fathers, bishops and imams.

b. **Society as a large community has its influences**: Societal values, beliefs, ideals and principles influences people's behavior, attitude and decision making. And people tend to follow societal trends in their decision making.

c. Government policy: This is another factor that influences decision making. Government laws, regulations, policies and restrictions guide people within the

government jurisdiction or territory. It is usually the pace which people under the government follow and any breach or contrary action is usually punishable. So people tend to make their decision in line with the laws and any breach or contrary action is usually punishable. So people tend to make their decision in line or correlation with that of government policies.

d. **Family values**: These are vital factors in influencing individual student's decision. The training or grooming of a child starts from the home (family). The values of the family have enormous or colossus effects in the life of a teenager/youth. Consequent upon this, good and moral value system of a family influences decision making of her members. Therefore, good family values are a recipe for good decision making for our teens/youths.

e. **Environment**: This is an evitable factor in decision making. Environment has substantial influences in our individual lives. Environment determines the way we talk, eat, relate with one another, the clothes we wear, how we greet one another etc. Environment defines our rules and boundaries etc. Therefore, the environment whether sick or healthy determines or influences our decision making processes and choices.

f. **Personal Preferences**: This is another important factor, because it is concerned about self and it is this self that feel the heat or effect of good or bad decision made. The individual values determine decision made on particular issues or actions. Notably, individual goals and career objectives influences his/her decision making process. Interestingly, while some families may have dirty and decadent values or behavior, it is on the discretion of an individual teenager to choose his/her lifestyle irrespective of his/her parents' lifestyle. For instance, a morally conscious student, whose father is the drunkard and smoker, could decide to choose a different course and lifestyle from that of his father. Again, a female teenager who has an unfaithful mother could also decide to be decent and morally sound.

g. **Friends**: Friends or one's friend could influence his/her decision making. Bad friends have negative influences on a teenager/youth. He/she could be induced or lured to engage in an activity, program or issue which he/she is not interested or does not value for. On the other hand, good and friendly company could facilitate good decision making and aid one in realizing his/her goals and career objectives.

h. **Available Information**: Information as noted earlier is very pertinent and efficacious to good decision making. Before crucial decisions are taken, it is important to take adequate measures to gain sufficient information that would guide good decision making process. There is no gain saying that knowledge is power.

i. **Feeling about Yourself**: Good feelings about yourself give you the confidence to tackle decisions. They also help you take an optimistic view of what is possible and even the impossible. On the contrary, when you feel down, you may avoid decision making and believe that the possibilities are limited. Striving to increase the good feeling you have about yourself can contribute to making better decisions.

j. **Resources**: Resources are everything available to you for use in managing your life. They may be anything from skills that you have to people, money, and tools. Often the decisions you make are affected by what resources you have and how well you recognize and make use of them.

k. **Pressure**: Sometimes, people try to take decisions away from you. They may use many different methods to influence your thinking. You need to be aware of the pressures that come your way and make your decisions on your own.

l. **Needs and Wants**: Many decisions are based on an evaluation of needs and wants. In general, needs must be met or fulfilled before wants. Better decisions are made when you know the difference between the two and choose accordingly.

m. **Values:** One of the most useful tools in decision making process is value system. People commonly turn to values to help them decide, ignoring appropriate values is a mistake.

How Are Decisions Often Handled?

Since people vary greatly, so do their reactions to the call for many kinds of decisions. Some people tackle decisions with careful confidence. Others, however, avoid making a decision or make them recklessly.

Procrastination

Sometimes, people simply procrastinate when faced with decisions. Procrastination means putting off. People who procrastinate recognize the need for decisions, but they choose to ignore or delay them for now and handle them later. People with poor management skill often put decisions aside. Sometimes people who procrastinate feel uncomfortable with making decisions. They may not have the confidence to face even small decisions head-on. Eventually, when a decision must be handled, problems can occur, fire brigade approach will now be required.

Denial

Failing to see that the need for a decision exists is another way of avoiding a decision. Even when strong evidence shows that some things needs to be done, the indications are ignore or even denied.

Sometimes decisions are difficult to face. Confronting them may mean handling emotions and situations that are unpleasant. A serious look at the possible consequences of avoiding the decision can often give people the strength to do what needs to be done.

Transference

Allowing others to make decisions for you is another type of avoidance. In these instances, the decision is transferred to someone else, and you must live with the results. Such decision making can be dangerous, especially if the decision has high impact on your life. If the person who controls the decision is unreliable, you are even more at risk.

Impulse Decision

Making a decision too fast can be just as troublesome as not making one at all. Impulse decisions are made quickly, without enough thought. Impulse decisions are usually more connected to wants than needs. They are often guided by emotions instead of reasons. In such situation, people may fail to think about what can happen afterwards. For instance, very serious consequences are possible for a person who chooses to be sexually active when the time and circumstances are not right. The prospects of pregnancy, contracting sexually transmitted infections (diseases), sinning against (destroying) his/her body and disobeying God may be overlooked when impulse overrules good judgment.

There is a fine line between making decisions with authority and making them too hastily. Often, people who can make quick, confident decisions are admired. The secret they have learned is, knowing how to evaluate impact. Dora knows how to do this. When a decision has low impact, she thinks quickly about what needs to be done and she takes a stand. For high-impact decisions, however, she is the first to say, *"I will have to think about it."*

Examining Your Skills

What kind of decision maker are you? You have read about all kinds of decisions and some related problems. Did you recognize yourself in any of this? If so, you may need to work on your decision making skills. At the very least, you can make some improvements.

Consequences of Making Wrong Decision:

- Regrets.
- Inability to meet goals.
- Loss of time.
- Not focused.
- Discouragement.
- Loss of self Esteem.

• Bad antecedent.

The importance of good decision making cannot be over emphasized. Good decision making facilitates achievement or accomplishment of one's goals.

COMMUNICATION AND INTER-PERSONAL SKILLS

"Many times a day I realize how much of my own outer and inner life is built upon the labors of my fellow men, both living and dead, and earnestly I must exert myself in order to give in return as much as I have received." - Albert Einstein

Communication is veritable and inevitable activity of human beings the world over. There is a saying that "Communication is the most important activity of man as every other thing depends on it" Amos asked in Amos 3:3 ***"Can two work together except they are in agreement"***. Communication is very important because people define us based on our utterances. Communication by definition is the expression of thoughts and ideas or making known ones ideas or feelings to another person or group of persons. Communication is at the heart of human interaction, because without it people cannot relate to one another. It is a process whereby a message is transferred from one person to another or to a group through verbal and non-verbal means. In addition, it is the process of exchange of information, message, ideas, attitudes, feelings and reactions.

Communication Channels

Communication channels refer to the various means by which information are disseminated. These include:

a. Verbal or oral means of communication

b. Non-verbal means of communication

c. Written communication

d. Visual means of communication

e. Intercom system Communication

f. Automated means of communication.

Verbal or Oral Communication

Communication, when it is verbal or oral, could be a face-to-face interaction between two or more person. This may be in the form of speech, conversation, inter-view etc. and a feedback is obtained simultaneously. Other examples of verbal/oral communication are:

a. Teaching during class lesson

b. Course during seminars and workshops

c. Meeting and conferences

d. Face-to-face conversation e. Telephone conversation

f. Radio and Television broadcast

g. Counseling and consultation.

Some of the Merits of Verbal Communication are:

• Feedback can be obtained instantaneously.

• It is possible to ask for clarification, so that the

Message, can be understood without

Misrepresentation, of facts.

• It is a direct medium of communication.

• Advantages of physical proximity and usually

Both, sight and sound of sender and receiver.

• Easier to convince or persuade.

• Verbal communication is also allows for

Contribution, and participation from all present.

However, Some of its Demerits Include:

• There may be no evidence or records of decisions reached.

• No source of future reference on information not written or recorded.

• Distortion of facts is possible in verbal communication.

• More difficult to hold ground in face of opposition.

• More difficult to control when a large number of people, take part.

• Lack of time to think right, as a result, decision made may be inferior.

Non-verbal Means Of Communication

The non-verbal means of communication consist of:

• Body Language: This is a means of transmitting messages, information, feeling or attitude through body signs or movement.

• Paralanguage: This is a means of transmitting Information, ideas and feelings through countenance, as in hissing to show displeasure, groaning to show pains. etc.

• Gesture and Distance Play a Great Role in non-Verbal Communication. The

following are non-verbal communication methods:

a. The clothes we wear.

b. The houses/rooms we live.

c. The way we sit or stand.

d. The way we shrug our shoulder or shake our head.

e. The way we twinkle our eyes.

f. Our facial gestures etc.

g. Eyes contact.

h. Sound of gums.

Written Communication

This refers to the document of oral communication into permanent records.

The written means of communication include:

a. Letter writing.

b. Internal memorandum used in meetings or formal gatherings/settings.

c. Text and exercise books.

d. Circulars.

e. Advertisements.

f. Invitation Cards.

g. Bulleting and periodicals.

h. Minutes of meeting.

i. Reports.

j. Statistical presentation.

k. School syllabus.

Advantages of Written Communication

a. It is an official form of disseminating information within and outside the family, school, church, organization etc.

b. It is a source for future reference. This facilitates decision making.

c. Agreement reached or decision taken is properly documented and cannot be denied or disputed.

d. It is capable of relating complex ideas, provides analysis, evaluates and summaries it.

e. It can also confirm, interpret and clarify oral communications.

Disadvantages of Written Communication

a. It is not possible to get immediate feedback since written message must reach the recipient before giving the necessary feedback.

b. Written communication if not guided can be misinterpreted.

c. Written communication can take time to produce and it is expensive.

d. Communication tends to be more formal and distant. Once dispatched, it becomes difficult to modify message.

e. it does not allow for exchange of opinion, views or attitudes except over period of time.

VISUAL MEANS OF COMMUNICATION

This is a means of illustrating information pictorially. Visual means of communication include:

a. Closed-circuit-Television, (CCTV) presents information verbally and pictorially

b. films and firm strip for educating recording tests, recruitment purposes, research, training etc.

c. Photographs.

d. Poster and notice boards.

e. Statistical graphs.

f. Wail Charts

g. Organizational Charts.

h. Drawings, diagram, cartoons and sketches.

Intercom System Communication

These include:

a. Telex and tele printer.

b. Facsimile telegraphic equipment (Fax), to facilitate the duplication of exact written, draw or typed records, between two distant points.

c. Pneumatic tube system: This is used to distribute papers to each department of an organization through the control station in a large container. The conveyor belt carries such document to the dispatch chutes for proper routing to the delivery points.

d. Electronic longhand transmission: This sends message by electronic items in one's handwriting.

e. Tele type-writer: this is used for transmitting written communication. A simultaneous reproduction of the message is typewritten on machines in another subscriber's location.

Advantages of Visual Communication

a. Reinforces oral communication.

b. Provides additional visual stimulus.

c. Simplifies written or spoken word.

d. Quantities provide ideas in number form.

e. Provides simulations of situations.

f. Illustrates techniques and procedures.

g. Visual communication also provides visual record.

Disadvantages of Visual Communication

a. Visual communication may be difficult to interpret without reinforcing written or spoken communique.

b. It requires additional skills of comprehension and interpretation.

c. It can be costly and takes time to produce.

d. It may be costly to disseminate or distribute.

e. Storage of visual communication materials may be more expensive.

f. Visual communication does not always allow time for evaluation.

Barriers to Effective Communication and Panacea

As noted earlier communication is vital to the survival of individual or group relationships. However, its purpose may be defeated by the following barriers if properly disseminated.

a. Lack of openness: The encoder attitude in communicating may lead to distrust. He/she may be perceived of or noted for hiding facts from the decoder. The encoder should let his/her 'Yes be yes' and "No be no".

b. Lack of enthusiasm either by the encoder or the decoder of information may lead to communication breakdown. The communicator should inject life into his message.

c. Assumption not clarified can also lead to communication breakdown. For instance, a teacher who informed the students to meet him in classroom, should state the particular classroom. Clarity of expression is essential in breaking communication barrier.

d. Badly expressed message on the part of the encoder. Poorly chosen words, omission, incoherent statements, jargons etc. can cause communication breakdown. The encoder should exercise greater care in disseminating information.

e. Lack of basic/fundamental knowledge of the subject matter is another cause of communication barrier. The communicator be should ascertain the knowledge of his audience in order to communication with them more appropriately.

f. Emotional reactions to situations as love, hatred, fear, happiness, sadness or anger would make communication very likely. The encoder should be calm before disseminating sensitive information.

g. Personality and appearance of the encoder could cause communication breakdown. People may not be willing to listen to him if he is too dirty or he/she looks unkempt. Dressing neatly and decently is a good way of gaining attention from prospective audience.

h. An unreasonable bias about the information being disseminated can create communication barrier. It is necessary to educate the recipient on the benefits accruable to them by following a specific line of action.

i. Distractions such as noise, inadequate illumination, provocative dressing, uncomfortable room, temperature etc. may create communication barriers.

j. Language could be a major barrier in communication. This could be a consequence of different interpretations. For examples, proceeds to an accountant is the profits realized from sales, whereas, proceed to a soldier indicates that he should 'advance;' wrong spelling, diction, wrong pronunciation etc., are some factors that instigate or facilitate communication barrier, it is necessary to avoid errors and correctly choose words. There is no offence in keeping our message short and simple.

Skills Required in Effective Communication

- Listening skills.

- Observation skills.

- Attention skills.

• Questioning skills.

Importance of Good Communication

Importance of good and effective communication cannot be over-emphasized. Some of them include:

a. It enables an individual to feel good about himself or herself.

b. It enables and individual to get along better with others.

c. Prevents misinterpretation or misunderstanding of information.

d. Prevents a breakdown in communication.

e. Helps to strengthen personal or group relationships.

INTERPERSONAL AND COUNSELLING SKILLS

Interpersonal communication is the communication between two or more persons. It is the ability of an individual (student) to initiate, articulate and express his/her views to one or more persons based on the context, idea or matter on hand. Interpersonal skill is needed for us to communicate effectively and efficiently in communication processes (which could between two individuals, group or congregation). The skill also enhances effective negotiation process. Interpersonal communication and feedback cannot be over stressed because it is inevitable in human relationships. On the other hand, counseling is one-on-one relationship between a counselor and the counselee to solve the counselee's problems, give advice or share ideas. A counselor is assumed to be knowledgeable in a particular field or profession before such a person could effectively counsel a client. In addition to his/her profession, a counselor needs certain skills like - listening, observation, questioning, reviewing, confidentiality and referral skills to do well.

Summarily, communication, interpersonal communication and counseling are important life building skills needed by youths and teens to respond and cope with life demands and challenges. We all make mistakes sometimes in our behavior, speech and actions.

(We all stumble in many ways. If anyone is never at fault in what he says he is a perfect man, able to keep his whole body in check, likewise the tongue is a small part of the body, but it makes great boasts). - James 3:2

GOALS AND GOAL SETTING SKILLS

"A concert violinist was asked why she was so successful: She answered, PLAN, then NEGLECT. Ignoring those things that take so much of our time and makes impossible for us to focus on the bigger issues of life and our own goals."

Accomplishing any goal in life is much like winning. Good feelings come when you set out to do, be, or accomplish something and you succeed. You have that winning and self-esteem or fulfilled feeling. Goals are the things, programs, activities or processes we want to achieve in life (it is usually our life objectives, aims and aspirations) towards which we direct our efforts (actions and inactions) and determine our successes in life.

Setting goals and the process of achieving these goals is very important in life. Whether you are planning daily, weekly, monthly, annual activities, or future career, understanding the proper steps in goal setting will help you not only in setting the goals but to achieve or attain them. Goal setting is the process of determining what 'goal' one wants or intends to attain. The goals we set depend largely on our values (that is what we consider to be important).

Types of Goals

There are basically, two kinds of goals short and long term goals.

1. **Short Term Goals**: These are goals; activities and/or programs to be achieved in a short period of time such as within days, weeks or few months. For instance, you want to improve in your performance and grades in a particular subject(s), terminal or promotion examination or vocational aptitude. First, you have to be determined, then, the steps will include setting a private time table for your studies and ensuring that no program, event, occasion or activity will stop or distract you from absolute concentration and comprehension. Then, consistency persistency and painstaking are very crucial to attainment of short term goals.

2. **Long Term Goals**: These are goals to be achieved over a long period of time like many months, years or over a life time. It involves series of activities, program

or processes to be undergone before they are attained. Some of these goals could be career oriented like been a doctor, an engineer, a nurse, a pilot, a geologist, a researcher/lecturer, a banker, a journalist, a broadcaster, a politician, a scientist, an administrator, a manager, an accountant, a lawyer, a pastor, a footballer, an athlete, a business mogul or tycoon and so much more.

Interestingly, short term and long term goals are interwoven, this is because achieving short term goals invariably translates to attaining long term goals. Accomplishing short term goals are gateway; recipe; or panacea to achieving long term goals. For example, a student who wants to be a pilot or an engineer will study hard enough to credit his/her science subjects convincingly without any form or nature of examination malpractices. Such a students must forget, or deny himself/herself some social programs or activities like partying watching movies and musical videos, hanging out with friends all times, and/or engaging in unnecessary and profitable or unproductive activities or programs that will add little or nothing to accomplishment of stated or outlined goals. Rather, he/she will painstakingly indulge in comprehensive and qualitative study which could be personal or group to improve or advance class lessons and studies to achieve better results through adequate and timely preparations. In this context, recommended and relevant text books are consulted and studied regularly to ensure optimum examination success. Consequently, such short term goal programs or activities now translate or metamorphose into achieving long term goal of been what you have set or determine for yourself.

Steps in Setting and Achieving Goals

There are steps in setting and achieving goals. Some of which includes:

- Clarify your underlying motives, that is, what are your interest and values? What do you want to be, or achieve? What are the things that motivates you?

- Identify your options, that is, consider your possible alternatives, what choices you have among the existing variables. You want to be a doctor, an engineer, a baker, banker or a lawyer? The choices are endless.

- Among these alternatives, make a choice, that is, chose or select the option or alternative that best fits your aspiration, interest and/or values.

• Set a reasonable time frame or limit. In this factor, your workload is reduced. This because your academic calendar or years of programs have been fixed or outlined by the education ministry or school authority. All you need to do is to work in line with the time frame already in place. This will help you to be at alert and be watchful as time waits for no man.

• Work consistently towards achieving your set goal (s). This is important because, it is not only necessary to set goals but to work tirelessly and assiduously to achieve such goals. In our individual lives, we have or encounter situations or challenges that could deter or makes us deviate or derail from our goals or objectives. Such factors include; peer pressure, economic meltdown/hardship or affluence (i.e. favorable and unfavorable economic conditions), family background, associations or mix-up with friends, social environment etc. These factors could make or mar your goals and objectives which in turn determine your successes or failures and consequently your relevance in the society. Your relevance in the society is determined by who you are and you contribution to the growth and development of your immediate environment, society and nation. There is saying that says "A good name is better than great riches."

• Because you are functioning with time, check progress routinely or periodically. This means that you evaluate yourself and performance from time to time through established results and evaluation tests, examinations results, interactive forum with friends, classmates, study group(s), teachers or parents as the case may be.

• Finish or conclusion. At this stage you can look back, front, sideways, and behold your achievements and beat your chest in satisfaction or fulfillment. Then congratulate yourself on your outstanding and distinguished achievement(s) or feat(s). Take the next step, set another tactical and achievable goal(s).

Importance of Goal Setting

Setting both short and long term goals has many advantages for you, your family, society and country at large. Here are a few of the ways goals add to life:

1. **Goals Gives Sense of Direction and Purpose:**

When you set goals, you give a purpose to your activities and programs. There is meaning to the way you spend your time. Having goals gives direction to your life. Goals can help you decide how to use your resources to get what you want.

"If you don't know where you are going, you will probably end up somewhere else." Laurence J. Peter

2. **Goals Motivate People:** To motivate simply means to cause people to act. While people without goals tend to get moving. A teen who wants to improve his/her academic performance would create extra time for studies. Some people are inspired to learn new skills or change old habits in order to reach their goals.

3. **Goals Promote Positive Feelings:** These feelings makes life more enjoyable and fulfilling. People who set goals and work to achieve them feel good about their goals, their accomplishments, and themselves. Reaching a goal proves that you can take charge and do what you set out to do. This builds confidence, which leads to further goal setting and further accomplishments in the future.

4. **It serves as a guide:** Goals serve as a guide that helps us make decisions about what we want to do and how to go about achieving them.

5. **It gives direction:** Goal setting meaning and direction to your activities.

6. **Goal setting facilitates or enhances success:** Goal setting increases our chances of successfully achieving our aspirations and career objectives.

7. **Goal setting enhances proper planning:** This is obviously true because when you set goals, you have indirectly and put programs and actions in appropriate places

Importance of Resources to Goal Attainment

Goals are of little use without resources. Resources are what enable people to turn goals into reality. Everyone talks about the resources of a country. These are the natural endowment, substance and features of the earth that can be used for different purposes. When the subject is goals, however, the term resources have a more specialized meaning. You read earlier that resources are all those things that you use to help manage your life. Resources can be divided into three main dimensions or kinds: Human, material and community/societal resources. Knowing all the resources available to you is an important part of achieving goals. Now, let us examine what those resources are:

• **Human resources:** These include the qualities that people have, such as knowledge, skills, talents and energy. Others are time available to you. People themselves can be resourceful, many have information and skills to share that can help you reach your goals. They also offer you their own time and energy For instance, your teacher, lecturer, counsellor or pastor can provide you needed information that could aid or facilitate your decision and actions. Your relations, friend(s), peer(s) or neighbor can be of help to you. These are harnessing of human resources available to you.

• **Material resources:** These consist of money and possessions. Money allows you to purchase whatever you want or need to attain certain goals. You might buy a text book, newspaper, or educative magazine to enhance your studies and knowledge. You might buy a phone, car a video game for your leisure or enroll in a computer programs. What goals might be associated with each of these purchases? Money can also be used to buy services that will help you reach your goals. For instance, for you to improve on difficult subjects or solve a particular problem like health, vocation etc. you might need to contract the services of an academic, medical or technical experts, to help you actualize your goal(s). Again, in planning to have a certain career, money buys training, books, uniform and/or tools of the trade or vocation.

Possessions are also resources used in achieving goals. If your goal is to have a good house, robust family, a good car, a good living and sufficient money to take care of your bills, then you must engage in meaning and profitable activity or programs. A student would need to study diligently and work extra hard in order to pass promotional examinations and crucially important, study a course or profession that will guarantee him/her a good pay. Other possessions can be equipment or supplies needed for performing specific tasks. Interestingly, I have come to realize that millionaires and billionaires don't work for people, rather they establish their own business empires and people come and work for them. They are not salary earners. They are entrepreneurs that set up chains of ventures. They are the bosses and people are answerable to them, they are the ones that issue instructions and they are obeyed. Bill gates, Opara Williams, Aliko Dangote, Mike Adenuga, etc. are cases in point. Think big but start small: A journey of one thousand (1,000) miles begins with a step.

• **Community resources:** Being aware of all your resources means looking beyond self, family and friends to the community. Every community has facilities and prospects or potentials that can be useful for reaching your goals. Facilities are places designed for a particular purpose, such as schools, libraries, stadia, general hospitals, museums, parks etc. You meet many of your educational, medical and recreational goals with these facilities.

Community resources include services as well as facilities. Community services can help you achieve goals.

Using Resources to Accomplish Your Goals

Knowing what your resources are is one thing, knowing how to use them is another. In the discussion below, you will discover how to get goals and manage resources to realize what you want to do.

Beat the procrastination trap.

Even after you have set your goal(s), procrastination can still be a problem, especially if the goal is a large or tough one. Wikipedia defines Procrastination as 'the counterproductive deferment of actions or tasks to a later time'. It can interfere with any stage of setting or reaching your goal. Here are some ways to overcome procrastination:

1. Begin by deciding on the smaller details. Write down when and where you will start the programs, activity or project as well as what tools, resources and information you will need.

2. Make a list of short, easy task that are related to achieving your goal and begin

with them.

3. Do least favorite jobs or duties before easier ones. Sometimes the hardest tasks are the most important ones in realizing your goals. Getting them out of the way will make the rest of the load or tasks seem lighter or easier. Also, if you put off unpleasant duties, you might accidentally run out of time for them.

4. Join or form a synergy with others who are pursuing the same goal. If you are putting off studying for a test or an examination, form a study group. Meeting regularly will not only force you to meet your goal, but also give you the added support of others along the way.

5. Promise yourself an appropriate reward after you have reached or accomplished your goal(s). Give yourself a little treat for achieving short term goals. Save large rewards for meeting major goals.

Management Process

Most life situations can be managed more smoothly if you are organized. Reaching goals is a good example. You are more likely to succeed if you an organized plan. You may also get more done. The management process is a system for managing goals and resources to get what you want in life. You can learn this system and make it of your routine. The process includes four basic steps that must be followed in the right order.

• Set a goal.

• Make a plan to achieve you goal based on the resources available to you.

• Carry out your plan for reaching or attaining your goal.

• Evaluate what happened in steps 1, 2 and 3 in order to learn from your experience.

Setting a Goal

Goal setting as noted earlier is the act of establishing a goal for yourself and/or your family. You decide what your goals will be and make it official so you will know what you are aiming for. The goal you choose to set will depend on your needs, wants, values and interests. You may have several goals that apply to different parts of your life. Some may be short-term and some long-term.

When you set each goal, try to be realistic. Ask yourself if you will be able to reach this goal with the resources available to you. If you set goals that you can't possibly reach or attain, you will likely become discourage and frustrated. Don't give up; believe in yourself, to give up is to give in. Nothing good comes easy; never say never to great and positive thing. Be passionate.

Although, a realistic approach is usually best, sometimes challenging goals can be set. After all, dreams can come true. Don't be afraid too after what you want. The different between I can and I can't is T. By working hard and gathering all possible resources, you may be surprised at what you can achieve.

When you set goals, set as much goals as you can handle, consider the amount of time and energy you have, think about the resources available. You may need to limit or refine your current goals and save the rest for a time when you will have the resources to succeed. Remember that with God at flings are possible: You can do all things through Christ that strengthens you. Once you have set a goal, write it down or inscribe it in your mind. Be specific and detailed about it. This will give you a clearer focus on exactly what you must do to attain it. And you will discover that with diligence and determination, you will make or accomplish it.

Becoming a Good Manager

As a teen or youth, you may have more opportunities to set goals of your own than you have ever had before. Sometimes teens and youths are discourage by what they see, hear, know or situations around them. They may have family problems or believe they lack the resources they need for a better future. One of the youths who felt this way made a decision. She said, "I can't change what happened yesterday, and today is not particularly good, but I can make tomorrow different." By setting goals, digging for resources, learning to make good decisions, and putting management skills into action, she is out to make a better future for herself and she did.

No matter what challenges you face, you can do the same. Now is the time to start asking yourself what you want for your future. You have a choice. You can think, plan, and act. On the contrary you can let circumstances take charge of your life. What will you choose?

In summary, goals are the things, programs, activities or processes we want to achieve in life (it is usual our life objectives, aims and aspirations), towards which we direct our efforts (actions and inactions) and determine our success in life.

Goal setting is the process of determining what 'goal' one wants or intends to attain. The goals we set depend largely on our values and interest. It helps you work towards achieving your life aspirations, and career. Although, there may be hurdles or obstacles to overcome, with determination and focus, you can persistently achieve your goals and objectives in life.

VALUES PLACING SKILLS

Values are beliefs, principles and standards to which we attach a lot of importance and want to keep or sustain. They are based on ideas about what is right, good and desirable. The set of values that you have is called your value system. How you spend your time, energy and money indicates your values. You choose certain activities over others; you choose clothes you wear, and words that reveal your attitude about what is important. You adopt qualities that you admire and feel are right for you. Together, all these make up your value system. As we grow up, we start to develop our own values which are influenced by family, role models, friends, society, environment, education, religion, etc.

Personal Values

Individuals have their values which defers from one person to another, however, there are some who correlate with one another. They include:

- Honesty
- Loyalty
- Respect
- Having friends/acquaintance
- Fashionable
- Helpfulness and generosity
- Empathy
- Good or qualitative education/meritocracy
- Religious/religion
- Nicety etc.

Families have value system too.

A family's value system is usually a blend of what family members believe. The adult in a family provide the foundation for the value system.

Influences on Values

Value systems are subject to changes and challenges. Over the years, new interests and concerns can cause some of your values to change. You will routinely find them challenged in many ways. It pays to be cautious as you absorb other ideas into your thinking. Friends have a strong effect on personal values. This is especially true during the teen years when value are being tried and tested. Although, you can learn from friends, sometimes there are pressures to go against what you value.

Your values are tested every day in many other ways. The media, movies, television, magazine and newspapers suggest all sorts of values, not all are good ones. Smoking and drinking are made to look appealing. Beauty and good looks are emphasized. Violence is a common theme. Your own good sense and a strong value system can help you resist such influences.

Families, friends and the media are not the only influences on values. Schools and teachers have an effect, too. Neighbors, community contacts, and religious training are other influences. Many of these can have a positive impact on your thinking.

Importance of Values and Value System

A strong value system can be a useful tool. Here are some of the ways it can be helpful to you:

- **A value system helps you make decisions:** The more difficult the decision, the more you need values to guide you. Values can reduce confusion in your life. When you know what is important to you, making choices is easier. For instance, declining drinking alcohol, going to an obscure place or meeting, etc.

- **Values provide motivation:** When something is important to you, you are likely to go after it. Knowing what you want can cause you to take action. You are much more likely to focus rather than drift in life. For example, if you value wealth or affluence, you will study hard, read a good course/discipline and get a profession/career that will pay you well or better still establish your own business empire or outfit. There is joy and fulfilment in being financially independent.

• **Values control behavior:** Positive values keep people from doing what they shouldn't. They place limitations on behavior. In other words, behavior of an individual falls in line with or are propelled by his/her values.

• **Clear values provide confidence and strength:** If you have ever been in a situation in which you didn't know what to do, you know that this brings a feeling of insecurity. When you have values that steer you, however, you are confident and secure.

• **Values bring consistence to your outlook and actions:** People know what to expect from your behavior that is reliable, it is more readily accepted by others.

• **Positive values enable you to focus on others, not just yourself:** As result of self-discipline and control you are in charge of your emotions. You are not easily moved by what you see. You know your 'limits and principles, cannot easily compromise. So for you, you know the things you can do or say. In this instance, you are concerned about others, since to a large extent you cannot speak for them. The focus is shifted from you to them.

Developing a Value System

Your value system has developed with the help of your family, moreover, you are increasingly influenced by people and events outside your family, however, values may seem to conflict at times. For this reason, you need to be prepared to preserve, defend, adjust and strengthen your value system. Good judgment will help you.

Here are some guidelines to use as you develop a value system that will serve you well throughout life:

• **Follow the rules of society:** Rules and laws were created from the experiences of those who have discovered that without order there will chaos and destruction. The rules of society are based on values that respect life, property, and truth. Thus, such acts as killing, stealing and cheating are not allowed. Taking the laws of the land seriously contributes to the strength of society. It also makes you a stronger, better, nice and responsible citizenry. People who respect, abide, obey and follow the laws gain respect, recognition and opportunities in the society.

• **Choose right over wrong:** Even though answers are not always clear cur, to you will often know deep inside what is right. Often it is tempting to push an important value to the side. Take time to think about, what is really best for you and others. Challenge what you see and hear before you accept it. If you are not sure, ask questions. Is it illegal? Will it be harmful or dangerous to me, my future or anyone else? Will I regret it later? Remember, bad or wicked acts or behaviors have nemesis.

• **Learn from others:** Observe what goes on around you. The mistakes and experiences of others can be helpful as you decide what to include in your value system. Talking to an adult you trust a family member, teacher or counsellor, for instance can also help you clarify your value principles.

• **Become aware of your values:** when you know clearly what your values are, they will be there when you need them.

• **Contribute to the family value system:** When you hold your family value in high esteem, you would not want or act to betray them. There is a universal saying that "Remember the son/daughter of who you are." This means or indicates that your family is known for dignity, diligence, honesty, respect, responsibility, God fearing, nicety, uniqueness and genuine. And acting or behaving contrary to your family beliefs and principles is seen as taboo and absurd. You are seen as a bad egg of the family. You attract hatred to yourself by people who detest your behavior and attitude. You throw yourself in bad light and easily become topic of discussion. Worse still, you create a bad image of the family and become a bad ambassador. It is your civic duty and obligation to contribute to your family and societal values.

Acting on Values

Values mean nothing without action that is, the way it is with values. First you learn and sort them. You are only honest if you act that way, even when no one is watching. You are only thoughtful if you pay attention to the feeling of others. No matter what you say, people will soon see your values through your behavior. As you examine your value system, ask yourself if your actions match your beliefs. If not, why?

What can you do to act on what you believe is important.

The same principle is true of a family value system. A family has the responsibility to teach positive values. You have the responsibility to help put those values into action.

It is will be a repetition or an overstatement to talk about societal values, because the moments our behaviors and attitudes are put right, coupled with good family values which is a product or custodian of societal beliefs, culture, ideals, principles, etc. Then you can be rest assured that our society will be a good place to live. Remember! Good people: Great nation. It begins with you!

BEHAVIOURAL SKILLS

"It is easy to stand with a crowd, but it takes courage to stand alone."

Behavior is define as a human conduct relative to social norms or a state of probation about one's conduct.

Types of Behaviors

Behaviors can be assertive, aggressive or non-assertive. It is imperative for us to understand the intricacies inherent in these behaviors.

Assertiveness

This means standing up for your rights without violating anyone else's. Assertive behaviors make you feel better about yourself, feel confident, take charge and control of the situation and respected by others. The outcome of being assertive is that:

- You do not hurt others being discreet.
- You gain or earn respect for yourself.
- Your rights and those of others are respected
- Everyone feels good.
- You are objective and unbiased.

Aggressiveness

This means you stand up for or act on your rights at the expense of someone else's. Aggressive behaviors make you and others feel angry, frustrated, bitter, guilty or lonely. The resultant effect of being aggressive is thus:

• You dominate an issue, talk or situation.

• You humiliate or embarrass some else.

• You win at the expense of others.

• You go home happy, while others are grieve or displeased.

"In the end, it is important to remember that we cannot become what we need to be by remaining what we are." - Max Dupree

Non-Assertive Behaviors (Passive)

This means giving up your basic rights so that others can achieve theirs. Non-assertive behaviors make you feel helpless, resentful, disappointed, dissatisfied and anxious.

The consequential effects of non-assertive behaviors include:

• You do not get what you want.

• You compromise so easily.

• Anger or grieve builds up in you.

• You feel lonely.

• You are always bias and subjective.

• Your rights are violated and trampled upon.

"Show the light and the people will find the way, the man who holds the light leads the way for the light is not concentrated at the feet of the holder"* - *Nnamdi Azikwe

Having highlighted or examined these behavioral traits. It is important to examine yourself, discover your own behavioral characteristics, then strengthen your opportunities and improve or work on your weaknesses or threats. Permit me to opine or assert that assertiveness is the greatest of these behaviors because, it earns you respect, confidence, makes you take charge and control, you neither hurt others nor trample on their rights. Most importantly, it guarantees your satisfaction and peace of mind. However, these behavior traits are dependent on the immediate situation or condition at hand. In other words, they have their purposes, but assertiveness offers us the personal power to manage and solve many of lives' problems.

Examples of each type of Behavior on the Analytical table:

NON-ASSERTIVE	ASSERTIVE	AGGRESSIVE
Tends to show a lack of appreciation for self	Tends to show appreciation for self and others	Tends to show Appreciation for self alone
Indirect / no expression of self	Honest and direct expression of self without infringing on their rights	Threatening, demanding, hostile expression of self
Hopes others will guess ones thoughts and feelings	Uses I message to to express thoughts and feelings	Uses YOU message to blame others

Places responsibility for making the decision on another person	Assumes responsibility of thoughts, feelings and behaviors	Assume little responsibility for the consequences of his Behavior
Always give in when a disagreement occurs	Compromises when necessary (without compromising values)	Always wants it his/her own way
Soft, uncertain voice, poor eye contact, fidget tense and poor posture	Clear and firm voice, comfortable eye contact, relaxed, good posture	Superior to no voice, overly direct eye contact, sharp, abrupt gesture, stiff
Believes he has to satisfy others need	Choose to satisfy others interest and his/ her own needs	Strives to satisfy only only self interest
Does not fight to win	Both parties win	Must win at all cost
Listens	Listens and act	Does not listen
Puts self down	Elevate self and others	Puts others down

An assertive person is in the best position to make a difference. Assertiveness is about going after mutually beneficial goals. The assertive person has better control of his/her emotions. He/she learnt to freely express his/her thoughts and has little or no 'carryovers' of emotional baggage. Consequently, he/she finds it easy to forgive, trust, correct and give advice. People are also able to easily accept his/her frankness because of the considerate manner in which he/she communicates with them.

Passive behavior does not have a long lasting influence on people. It often results in frustration and sudden emotional outbursts. A passive person tends to bottle up his/her emotions, gets taken for granted to the extent that, a seemingly inconsequential event triggers off a violent reaction.

Just like the case of passive behavior, aggressive behavior does not achieve a long-lasting transformation. People may respond to an aggressive individual out of fear, but they are not influenced on a mental level. An aggressive person exhibits a high level of 'phoniness' in his/her dealings, readily violating his 'principles' when he/she find it expedient to do so. His/her primary aspiration is to win at all costs.

Specific Aggressive and Passive Behavioral Styles

Described below are some categories of people who may be considered as difficult.

- **Fault Finder:** Highly judgmental persons and takes great pleasure in finding faults with people.

- **Blamer:** Passes on the blame for his/her failures and predicaments on other. For instance, it is common among mediocre students to pass on blames or reasons for their failures in examination/test to the teacher, examiner or authority/body that conducted such examination. They don't see anything wrong in their attitudes towards the examination/test. They fail to study and prepare adequately for such examination. Even when they know, they pretend that all is 'well', when in reality all is not well.

- **Parasite:** The 'modus operandi' (a particular method of working or doing things the usual way) is to do very little for the greatest result. He/she does not contribute to teamwork but wants to share fully in the credit. He will never work hard but seeks for ways to use others.

• **Shredder:** He sees people as objects to be torn apart. He enjoys rebuking people in public.

• **Poison Gasser:** Always seeking a diplomatic way of passing on information that is injurious to an individual or a group of people.

• **Bomber:** Unlike the poison gasser, he is bold and loves confrontation. He/she openly attacks people. He/she promotes group or individual warfare (bringing or causing quarrel between persons or people).

• **Slave Driver:** Sees the task as the only paramount issue in every situation, downplaying the emotions of the people who do the work.

• **Total Adviser**: Has a solution to every problem and wants to advise everyone on the right course of action to take in every situation.

• **Comparer:** Very jealous and envious of others and will constantly pass derogatory remarks.

• **The Rock:** Stubborn and may be arrogant, refusing to see issues from others' point of view

• **The Soul of the Party:** He strives for all the attention and gets uncomfortable when someone else takes Centre stage. He/she may even attempt to damage the image of a person who is in the limelight.

• **Nice Guy:** This is the most unusual type of difficult behavior. He/she is very nice and deliberately seeks to be in the good books of everybody. It really gets to him/her when negative statements are made about him/her. He/she may be dishonest in relationships in an attempt to always look good.

Food for Thought

1. Which of the traits described above do you recognize in yourself?

2. How can you change?

3. How can you help others, who have similar traits, to change?

"It is dangerous to suppress a negative feeling or bad habit. It is better to recognize it and cultivate its opposite virtue through mediations, affirmation and prayer. In addition, we must strive to act the virtues we meditate upon, affirm and pray for!" - Obafemi Awolowo

NEGOTIATION AND REFUSAL SKILLS

"Behind every noble lift, there are principles that have fashioned it." - George H. Lorimer.

Negotiation is a discussion aimed at reaching an agreement. It allows people to solve a problem, resolve a conflict amicably or reach an agreement. It is important to learn how to negotiate in our daily lives and relations with other people. This is because, callous people aim or intend to manipulate and outsmart us and take advantage of our weakness and ignorance, to their own benefit and to our detriment. It is therefore, pertinent that we acquire skills to enable us meet our needs without anyone feeling guilty, angry, cheated or intimidated. Again, when negotiation is used effectively, it enhances relationships. Notably, factors like age, gender, socio-economic empowerment influence effective negotiation.

Skills Required For Effective Negotiation

1. **Effective communication skills:** Speak using clear and simple words and sentences so that it is easy for the other person to understand your intention(s). Using positive body language (such as smiling and looking at the other person while talking or speaking to him/her) can help you communicate your intention(s) even more effective.

2. **Listening skills:** Listening carefully to what another person is saying is very important. Use positive body language (such as smiling and nodding of head) to show that you understand what he/she is saying or has said. Unless, such subject matter is a 'no go area'. Ask questions if you don't understand or needs further clarification. Don't swallow or subvert your views or submission on the matter. Don't pretend to have understood what the other party said when in fact you are lost in the discussion or conversation. Don't compromise your position or view especially when it matters or crucial that you talk or speak. This is because people tend to look down on you, when in a situation, meeting or discussion, you are

expected or ought to speak and you decline. Unless you specify or comment the reason(s) for your action.

3. **Observation skill:** Carefully observe the other person's non-verbal intentions/clues while both of you are speaking. These non-verbal clues can be positive body language, such as nodding to show that they understand what you are saying or negative cues such as looking around or doing other things which could show that they are not listening.

4. **Critical thinking skill:** Having listened to and observed the other person's intentions through communication, carefully weigh the implications of their statements, exposition or submissions. Engage in logical reasoning and read meaning into the verbal communication and body language.

5. **Peer resistance skill:** Use of nice attitude and positive body language will further help you to communicate your intentions. Be objective and assertive in your opinion; let both your oral speech and body language drive home your points.

6. **Problem solving skill:** Ability to quickly think out a solution to a problem would earn you more respect. For instance, in a class or meeting, your ability and willingness to contribute positively and brilliantly would make your peers to acknowledge you some respect. People especially your peers would always wish to identify with you because they believe you have something to offer. When you are endowed or gifted with first class brain, that is, high intelligent quotient (IQ), genuine people would want to relate and associate with you. However, if in your self-evaluation or assessment, you realize that you are an average student, you can improve or enhance your intelligent quotient to the level of first class student/distinction. This requires hard work, focus, determination, persistence and diligence. Consistent or regular and comprehensive study of text books and lesson/lecture notes will improve an average student to first class or distinction candidate. Remember, "Study to show yourself approved" according to Timothy.

Another way of acquiring problem solving skills is for students to always engage in research and innovative (creative) ventures. Always try to do an unusual thing. Reading widely is also very useful, aside reading your text and exercise books; it is brilliant to read newspapers, success stories of Icons and Legends of our time, inventors and inspirational leaders of the world. Knowledge acquired from such stories or biographies could 'ginger your swagger' to do something positive, unique and exceptional, which in turn, will benefit you, your family and the society. People like President Barack Obama, Bill Gates, John Kennedy, Nelson Mandela, Mother 8Theresa etc. are personalities people yearn and aspire to be like.

Good negotiation skills are important as problems and conflict of interests will always present themselves. To every problem, there may be more than one solution, but the necessary factor is that the solution is agreed between the parties concerned and is mutually beneficial to them.

(For the LORD gives wisdom; out of His mouth Come's knowledge and understanding. When Wisdom enters into your heart and knowledge is pleasant unto your soul). - Pro. 2:6, 10

Refusal Skills

Refusal skills can be defined as the ability of an individual to disagree with a situation or condition that is not favorable or conflicts with his/her interest. It is a decline or refusal to yield to request by another person by saying 'No'. This assertion should be understood and clear to the person advancing the request.

Situations Where Refusal Skills Are Applied

Conditions in which an individual person is expected to exhibit refusal skills include:

• Being offered an alcoholic drink and/or drugs.

• Being offered a stick or pack of cigarette

• Being offered a diet pill as an overweight or obese person.

• Being pressured to have' a sexual relationship.

• Being influenced or induced to steal or tell lies.

Differences between Negotiation and Refusal Skills

With negotiation skill, one will affirm reasons convincingly why a particular position, opinion or decision is maintained.

There are however, some elements of compromise in negotiation, this is because as you negotiate with the other party, there must be some level of disagreement which while negotiating would be brought to bear and considered. And in the interest of peace, mutual interest and agreement, a particular decision is reached.

Whereas, with refusal skills, one does not compromise his/her position or affirmation on a matter of interest. Your decision is made discreetly and absolutely to your partner or negotiator.

Maintaining the position of non-comprise can be achieved by not advancing reason, for taking a position or decision. Thus, you cannot get convinced as a result of counter argument that the other person may present. Your objective living and unbiased decision or opinion would enable you not to be responsible of attendant consequences that may result in the course of or aftermath of the activity, action or program. In other words, let your no be "NO" both in speech and body language.

Steps in Demonstrating Refusal Skill

1. Talk about the issue, the situation and what your stand point is. Say "No" with words like "I don't want to have sex now or anytime soon until I'm married "I don't want to join the group, they are bad influences or occultist's". "I don't want to smoke it is dangerous to my health and can make me die at a tender age of my

life".

2. Say "No" with your body and your entire non-verbal attitude, make eye contact that says "NO."

3. Stand back from the person who is pressurizing you, especially if it is sexual pressure, this will give confidence not to be trapped or wooed into doing it against your will.

4. Keep repeating "NO" without giving any excuse or reason. This is because your partner or negotiator could be tricking you by asking such questions as "why do you say no?" 'Why are you afraid?" "You think I will hurt you?" "Others are doing it" "I will be careful". All these are rubbish. As a matter of fact, not everybody is promiscuous, unscrupulous and dirty, look at him/her discreetly and say "No."

5. Turn the conversation around and let him or her know how you feel about being pressured into doing something contrary to your principles and values and which is not in your best interest, the action which might ruin your life.

6 Leave the location, or refuse to discuss the matter anymore and walk away necessary or need be.

SKILLS IN DEVELOPING A GOOD SELF-ESTEEM

"Man cannot live without some knowledge of purpose of life, if he can find no purpose in life, he creates one in the inevitable of death." -Chester Himes

This is a reflection of one's self-worth. It could be positive or negative, that is, high or low. It is positive (high) self-esteem when you see yourself in a positive way; accepting your strengths and weaknesses. On the contrary, it is negative (low) self-esteem when you do not see yourself in a positive way and focus more on your weaknesses. Notably, having a positive Self Esteem does not mean that you behave as if you are better than other people; rather it means that you have accepted yourself as you are based on a proper estimation or judgment of who you are. In other words, self-esteem is concerned with the ability of a person to have confidence in himself/herself, having the spirit of I can do it; I can try it; I can make it.

High self-esteem people have great and courageous hope in themselves. Whereas, low self-esteem persons are most times hopeless, they do not believe that every problem has a solution, and that certain problems are challenges meant to exact courage, intellectual abilities and wisdom in them, such persons lack courage and enthusiasm.

In this category of persons, the high esteem persons believe that whatever that happens to them is as a result of their action(s) or inaction(s). A high self-esteem person believes that his/her destiny is in his/her hands and with diligence and hard work through divine inspiration and direction he/she achieves it, while a low self-esteem person believes that the realization of his/her destiny is by chance. They use such words as 'what must be must be'. This is true but, faith without work is dead.

Another, interesting trait or characteristic attribute of self-esteem individuals is the believe that all that happen around and within them is as a result of internal factors which they must have firm control of. In other words, their successes or achievements are consequent upon their strengths and efficacious harnessing of their opportunities, and failures are resultant effects of their weaknesses and treats. They also take responsibilities of their actions whether favorable or unfavorable. In contrast, low self-esteem people are of view that whatever happens within and around them is against the backdrop of external factors that are not within or beyond their control. Their success or achievements are attributed to chance and their little efforts. They hardly work hard, because their opinion is that success is not measured by the parameter of their hard work. They shift their failures or problems (challenges) to external forces or witchcrafts; they believe that somebody somewhere is remote controlling and limiting them. Low self-esteem persons easily give in or commit suicide. They are easily depressed and allow unfavorable situations to oppress them. They easily get frightened in every little thing, even cockroach or ants scare them, and they give interpretations or connotations to such. For instance, when low self-esteem people fail examinations/tests, they attribute their failures to either the body /institution that conducted the examinations/test or the examiner that marked their papers/examined them. You could hear them say, they failed me, or that interviewer was wicked he/she intentionally failed me." They forgot or fail to realize the fact that such body rarely or doesn't know them. They also fail to understand that their successes or failures are consequent upon their effective or ineffective studies and preparations.

Understand Who You Are!

"Self-knowledge is best learned, not by contemplation, but by action. Strive to do your duty and you will soon discover of what stuff you are made." - Johann Goethe

A story is told of a farmer who enjoyed watching two eagles fly near a distant hill. When he did not see the eagles for a couple of days, he went to investigate. He found an abandoned nest that held an egg, which he took back to the farm. He placed the egg in a nest in a hen-house with a faint hope that it might hatch and eventually grow to become a matured adult eagle and fly.

Two weeks later, the egg hatched and the strange-looking baby eagle joined the chicks in the yard of the hen-house. As the first few days passed, the eaglet learned the habits of the chickens, eating the corn provided by the farmer.

Noticing some birds flying overhead one beautiful morning, the eaglet remarked, "Wouldn't it be wonderful to fly like that! I wish I can fly." But you know chickens do not fly; they quickly admonished her for that foolish thinking. "You are a chicken," they said, "You can't fly" The fearful mother hen said, "If you try to fly, you will surely get caught in the chicken wire and break your neck."

The strutting rooster father added logically, "Even if you flew over the fence, it would be hard to find food and you will probably starve." All the chickens agreed that the baby eagle should not try to fly.

"It sure would be wonderful to fly and soar like that," the eaglet repeated to itself. "I wish I could do it." But he did not try because he believed the chickens. As the days and weeks passed, the eaglet said little about flying. But it spent more and more time alone, often in the hen house.

Then one day, the farmer noticed that the eaglet was no longer in the chicken yard. He hoped the eaglet had grown big enough to fly away, but still searched around for it. The hen house was dark, and when he turned on the light, he noticed a clump of dark feathers in the corner. He went over, picked it up and saw that it was young eagle. Unfortunately, it was dead!

Apart from the eagle's inability to discover its true identity, the point is that allowing the world to tell you who you are or what you can do, without personally striving to discover your identity, can depreciate your self-worth.

Reflecting On Who You Are

"An ounce of experience is better than a pound book of knowledge." - Sierra Leonean proverb

My dear, I did like to suggest that you find a quiet moment, or go on a personal retreat to reflect on the following sets of questions. I encourage you to add more questions that apply to your peculiar situation as they occur to you.

Your thoughts:

What do you think about most of the time? What do you think of yourself? How do you think of others? How has your thought pattern changed over the years? Have your thoughts changed in the direction you desire or in the opposite direction?

Relationships:

How have you related with people over the years? How do you relate to people now? Do you encourage people or discourage them? Do you usually blame or develop people? Are you temperamental, contentious, perhaps unforgiving, impatient, and self-focused? How do you communicate with people? Are you domineering or understanding? Are you long-suffering, kind and forgiving? Do you sincerely care about others? Do you relate to people based on what you can get from them? Do you always seek for recognition? Are you a good follower? Are you loyal to a particular individual or the authority as a whole?

Vision:

What type of vision do you have regarding various aspects of your life: Family, spiritual, career, social, physical, mental, and finances? What short and long term goals have you set for yourself? Are you self-focused, or do you desire to make impact in the lives of others? Are you pursuing those goals? How do you react to challenges you face on the way? Do you get easily overwhelmed or are you persistent? How many goals have you set for yourself in the past and how many actually have you been able to achieve?

Your' Principles:

What is your attitude towards various aspects of your life? How much value have you added to what you do? How well do you work with your friends, people or colleagues? Are you a builder or destroyer? Are you loyal to the authorities? Do you seek to improve your performance on every occasion? Are you reactive? Do you seek solutions rather than focusing on the problem? Do you gossip? Do you backbite?

Your' Interest:

What are your interests? What are you passionate about? What do you do that you realize is not good for you? What do you do that you need to do more often? What makes you fulfilled? What makes you unfulfilled? How can you plan and reflect better?

Your' Resources:

What is your perception of the resources you possess? Do you see yourself as an owner or a custodian? If you have to give an account on a periodic basis, how well will you fare? How well do you manage your time, body, finances and talent? Are you building or destroying what you have? Do you think of how others can benefit from your resources?

Please note that it is important to remain objective as you spend your time reflecting on these questions. Your answers should help you to make a better connection with the issues raised in this piece of work.

"At creation, certain things were deposited inside of you to make you a success on planet earth. There is something inside that is able to answer the questions of life. There is a treasure in your nature that is able to terminate all your pressures in life. Until you know it, your struggle continues. The treasure is what I call talent." - David 0. Oyedepo

Your uniqueness stems largely from the gift that you possess. You can at use this uniqueness to make a difference in different undertakings. Someone with the gift of teaching and becomes a trainer is more positioned to excel in that area Your or sphere than others who are not similarly blessed. In their b, 'Discover God Given Gifts,' Don and Katie Fortune stated that we all have one or more out of seven types of gifts. The gift(s) with which we have been blessed "shape our personalities." They explained that a gift is a "Particular spiritual talent, of a gracious divine endowment," which we are supposed to use for the benefit of others or to achieve our purpose. They categorized these gifts as:

1. Perceiver: Clearly perceives God's will

2. Server: Loves to serve others

3. Teacher: Loves to research and communicate the truth

4. Exhorter: Loves to encourage others to live a victorious life

5. Giver: Loves to give time, talent, energy and means to benefit others

6. Administrator: Loves to organize, lead or direct

7. Compassionate Person: Shows compassion, love and care for those in need.

In the latter part of their book, they also described the types of careers for which people with certain gifts are best suited. For instance, they stated that a 'Giver' and an 'Administrator' are likely to succeed as business owners, whereas, someone with a gift of compassion may not do well at that. A 'Compassionate' person and a 'Server' may excel as a childcare provider but an 'Administrator' may just be average in that role. A 'Perceiver' has a high probability of successes a guidance counsellor and lawyer, while a 'Server' has limited chances. An 'Exhorter' is more likely to succeed as an occupational therapist and guidance counsellor; however a 'Giver' may not do well in that role.

The identification and effective use of your talent(s) /gift(s) will increase your level of success. And the identification of the gift of others and doing all within your reach or power to help them use the gifts will enhance your leadership effectiveness.

You will need to 'drive' your gift by using it. The more you drive a high performance car, the better it performs. Your position in life may not give you the opportunity to show case your talent/gift but you don't really need to wait for the 'right time.' You can decide to create the opportunities to encourage and motivate others either formally or informally. After all the gift of a man makes a way for him.

Characteristics or Attributes of Low Self-Esteem and High Self-Esteem People

The characteristic features of high self-esteem and low self-esteem people include the following:

High Self-Esteem;

- Assertive
- Confident
- Caring attitude
- Interactive• Respects authority
- Firm / bold

Low Self-Esteem;

•Arrogant / Proud

•Critical attitude

•Suspicious of people

•An inferiority complex

•Rebellious

•Allows self to be pushed around

Strategies for Improving Self-Esteem

An individual must be proud of and appreciate himself/herself irrespective of his/her weaknesses or disabilities before people could appreciate and respect them. We must realize that every individual has uniqueness endowed in him/her, People who think badly of themselves often adopt bad habits and negative attitudes. Therefore, some of the following strategies are veritable and pertinent in enhancing and improving self-esteem. They include:

• Accept yourself the way you are. Appreciate the nature in which you have been made. Be confident about yourself and your prospects. Have the `I can do it/I can make it spirit.' Believe in yourself even when people don't believe in you. Be patient with yourself.

• Set goals for yourself; strive to accomplish those goals so that you gain confidence in yourself and in others. Harness your God given potentials and encourage yourself in the midst of failure or opposition. For instance, in the 2010 FIFA world cup hosted by South Africa, Spain lost their opening match against Swaziland , but went on to win the competition. Even though they were among the world cup favorite, many people wrote them off after that first encounter. It shows that failure is not the end of the road, rather it is a prerequisite to restructure or re-strategize. Same are the issues of life.

• Prepare for challenges, because preparation is the key to triumph. Make preparation for success as well as alternative plans (plan B) in case of failure or disappointment. In it all, be focused, courageous, determined and persevere.

• Engage in positive things, exhibit positive attitudes and behaviors improve your image, be nice, and amiable.

• Use your family and friends who believe in you as a support system.

• Be bold, firm and assertive when your friends or group members try to intimidate or influence you negatively.

• Make decisions to change or improve what you do not like or appreciate about yourself. Be conscious of your weaknesses and threats. And make effective and judicious use of your strengths and opportunities.

• Very importantly, appreciate and reward yourself on your successes/achievements.

Conclusively, it is very pertinent and indispensable for young people to have clear values that reflect what they do and say. Having clear values means, you are not easily affected by peer and societal pressures. You are not easily moved by things that are contrary to your views and values. Building high self-esteem is a necessary skill which helps you to live a normal and successful life, helping you overcome peer pressure and developing positive attributes (strengths).Whereas, negative attitudes and behavior manifest weaknesses. Low self-esteem results in lack of courage, hope, determination focus and direction.

SKILLS IN DEVELOPING A GOOD ATTITUDE

"A conclusion is the place where you get tired of thinking" - Edward De Bono

Attitude is the way you see yourself in the milieu or perspective, of the larger world. It is the totality of your thought, understanding, beliefs and feelings.

Norman Vincent Peale, author of The Power of Positive Thinking, told the story of a young man in Boston who responded to a vacancy advertised in a local paper. When there was no reply, he decided to go to the post office and waited there for someone to collect the mail. He followed that person to an office, went inside, asked to see the manager and told him what he had done. The manager, though astonished, told him that they were always looking for people with perseverance and determination. He instantly gave him a job and that was how Roger Robinson, who later became a famous financier, got his first job.

A story is also told of a young man who went into a shop and came out with a tattoo on his arm that stated: Born to lose. He looked and acted like a loser. He is likely to have a reason for the tattoo. It will take a divine intervention and a major initiative for him to turn out to be a winner. Most people may not have tattoo on their arms, but on their minds. Who you think you are, is most likely to be who you will turn out to be.

Moods as Distinct from Attitude

A lot of individuals tend to judge their desires or passion based on their moods. People even judge others based on the observed moods. Unfortunately, mood is transient in nature, while an attitude is longer lasting. A bad MOOD, most times, is just a case of being 'Mad over Odd Desires.' The desire is 'odd' because we often wish things would happen in unrealistic or impractical ways.

Building the Right Attitude: Power of Expectations

Nell Mohney in her book, 'Beliefs Can Influence Attitude', recounts an experiment in which the principal of a school held a meeting with three of his teachers and told them that they were going to be given ninety (90) high intelligent quotient (IQ) students to work with because they were the best teachers in the school. "We are going to let you move these students through the next year at their own pace and see how much they can learn," he told them. Over the next one year, these ninety (90) students were learning from the 'brightest teachers' and the teachers too were teaching the 'brightest students '. They were all happy with the arrangement. By the end of that academic year, the students had achieved more than all the other students in the whole district.

At the end of the year, the principal had another meeting with the teachers where he made an amazing confession to them: "You did not have ninety (90) of the most intellectually bright students in the school this past year. They were actually just average students. We just chose ninety (90) students at random from the system and have them to you to teach." The teachers replied, "This means we must be exceptional teachers." But the principal's reply was, "I have another confession to make. You were not the brightest teachers in the school. Your names were the first three names drawn out of the hat." The astonished teachers asked, "What made the difference? Why did ninety (90) students perform at such an exceptional level for a whole year?" The difference, of course, was simply the 'pre-programmed' expectations of both the teachers and students!

When you have the right expectations, you somehow tend to always see possibilities rather than limitations. You are programmed to focus on opportunities rather than obstacles. You are able to first ask yourself where you went wrong before trying to determine where others may have gone wrong.

Changing Your Attitude

The indispensable concern or issue in changing your attitude is changing the way you think. To rethink your thoughts, you will need to pause for a few minutes and answer the following questions:

- What do I think about most of the time?
- What may be responsible for my thoughts?
- Why do I think about what I think about?
- When and where do I think about certain things?
- How can I improve my thought?
- WHY should I think to improve?

Thinking About Your Behavior

- How do I behave in certain situations and with various people?
- Why do I behave the way I behave?
- What thoughts influence my behavior?
- How should I think to improve my behavior?
- WHY should I act to improve?

Thinking About Your Communication

- What do I communicate in various situations?
- Is there a pattern to how I speak?
- What factors influence my speech and other forms of communication?
- How do I want to speak and why?
- WHY should I seek for positive change?

You can add more questions. The point of the exercise is to continually challenge your thought process through a personal self-analysis to see how you can move to the next level.

Psychologists have explained that it normally takes several weeks to change an attitude or develop a new habit. A few have said that it takes about twenty-one (21) consecutive days of doing the same thing continuously to be able to change a habit. Once a familiar momentum and trait has been broken, the mind adjusts to the new condition. The implication of this is that if you desire to change, you should persist, in repeating the same positive action for a certain period until it comes naturally to you.

ABOUT THE AUTHOR

Emma Pentool is a carrier building coach to teens, youths and adults. He is also a copywriter, book reviewer and a professional proofreader....

www.ingramcontent.com/pod-product-compliance
Lightning Source LLC
LaVergne TN
LVHW060838170826
845678LV00007B/1810

* 9 7 9 8 8 4 3 8 3 8 3 1 7 *